Fu... Home –
Animal
Adventures

Andy Blackford

Illustrated by Sole Otero

Contents

OXFORD
UNIVERSITY PRESS

Verona and the Sheep from Space

It was Monday morning at school.

'Wasn't it a lovely weekend?' said Miss. 'Jack, what did you do?'

'I went to the zoo, Miss!' said Jack. 'There was a lion.'

'Very good!' said Miss. 'And what about you, Verona?'

'I was abducted by aliens, Miss.'

Everybody laughed. Miss frowned. 'Now then, Verona – we don't tell fibs, do we?'

'I'm not fibbing,' she replied. 'I was in the garden and their spaceship landed right next to me.'

The rest of the class were nearly crying with laughter, but Miss was cross. 'Very well, Verona. So what were these aliens like?'

'Sheep, Miss.' There were more howls of laughter from the class. 'All sheep are aliens, Miss. They came to Earth from outer space, ages and ages ago.'

Miss' face went red. This was always a bad sign.

'All right, Verona! If you know so much about space travel, why don't you stand at the front and tell the class all about it?'

'Thank you, Miss,' said Verona. And she began her amazing story.

A very long time ago, the sheep that lived on the planet Clovenhoof knitted a spaceship out of wool. They visited all the nearby planets looking for other sheep, but there weren't any.

Finally, they reached Earth. It looked very inviting – blue, blue water and green, green grass.

'This is the one, lads!' cried the Captain. 'I can feel it in my bones!'

So they landed in a field near Bristol and set off to explore. And that's when it all went wrong.

This weekend

Verona stopped. The class weren't laughing anymore; even Miss wanted to know what happened next. 'Carry on, Verona!'

'I'm afraid it rained,' said Verona sadly.

Miss was puzzled. 'I don't understand.'

'The spaceship was made of wool,' Verona explained, 'so when it got wet, it shrank. Soon it was so small that the sheep couldn't get back inside.'

'So what did they do?' demanded Miss.

'I'll tell you,' replied Verona.

The sheep were upset. 'Let's radio for help,' one suggested.

'Don't be daft,' said the radio operator. 'The radio's inside the ship.'

'Don't worry,' said the Captain. 'We'll bump into some local sheep soon. I'm sure they'll lend us a radio if we ask nicely.'

But the sheep from Clovenhoof didn't realize they were the only sheep in the universe.

Instead, they bumped into some humans.

'Hello!' called the Captain in Sheepish (the language spoken by sheep). 'We are travellers from a distant galaxy and we wish you no harm. Take us to your leader!'

But the humans didn't understand. They just rounded up the sheep and shaved off their wool.

And it's been the same ever since.

The class went quiet. Finally, Miss said, 'That's a very sad story, Verona.'

'It could have been worse,' replied Verona. 'They could have bumped into wolves.'

'But Verona,' said Miss, 'you still haven't told us how you were abducted.'

'I was coming to that, Miss,' replied Verona.

I was playing in my garden when I heard a great *whoosh*. I was knocked off my feet by a huge wind. There was so much smoke and noise, I could hardly tell which way up I was.

Then the noise stopped and the sun came out again. And there, on the lawn, was a huge, woollen spaceship.

It was yellow, green and brown; and knitted in a pattern called Fair Isle, which is the official pattern of the Clovenhoof Star Fleet.

A door opened in the side of the ship and a sheep's head appeared. 'Greetings!' it said, in a Welsh accent. 'We are travellers from a distant galaxy and we wish you no harm.'

'Well, I don't think my dad will agree,' I replied. 'You've burned a big hole in his lawn.'

'Oh dear,' said the sheep. 'I'm terribly sorry. I'm afraid we've landed in the wrong place.

We're looking for a town called Abergavenny. We've brought the post from Clovenhoof.'

'Pardon me?' I said. I hadn't the faintest idea what he was on about.

The sheep stared at me. Then he said, 'Oh, look – we can't talk like this. Hop aboard and I'll explain.'

The inside of the ship was very homely and comfortable. Several sheep were relaxing on rugs. One of them seemed to be knitting a door!

'What's your name?' enquired the first sheep.

'Verona,' I told him. 'What's yours?'

'We don't really have names,' said the sheep. 'We all look so alike, we'd never remember who was who. But you can call me Barry if you like. Can I offer you a drink?'

I nodded. 'Yes please.'

'Milk or water?'

I wasn't sure what sheep's milk would taste like, so I went for the water.

'I expect you're wondering why we're here,' began the sheep. 'Pull up a crew member and I'll explain.'

I stretched out on a very fleecy sheep; she didn't seem to mind at all. Then Barry told me the strange story of how sheep first came to Earth ...

... 'So twice a year,' he concluded, 'we bring letters from the folks at home. We take them to the Sheep Post Office in Abergavenny. It's been this way ever since we conquered Earth.'

'It doesn't sound as if you conquered anyone!' I said.

'That depends on how you look at it,' Barry smiled quietly.

I asked him, 'Aren't you worried in case it rains? Abergavenny is in Wales, you know. Wales isn't exactly famous for its scorching sunshine.'

'We're very careful nowadays. We always check the weather forecast first – and we try to avoid humans! In fact, on Clovenhoof we have a song:

Baa baa black sheep, have you any wool?
No sir, no sir,
And now if you don't mind,
We really must be going.'

Barry glanced at a large, woollen sundial.
'Goodness! Is that the time? We'll never find
Abergavenny in the dark.'

I got up from my sheep. 'Sorry I kept you. Thank you for telling me your story.'

'It's a pleasure!' replied Barry, and he handed me a package. 'I would be honoured if you would accept this small gift from the sheep of Clovenhoof.'

As the door swung shut, Barry waved a friendly hoof. 'Goodbye, Verona!' he said. 'Sorry about the lawn!'

Then there was a lot of smoke, wind and noise, and the spaceship rose slowly into the air and thundered away towards Wales.

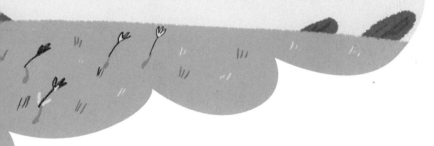

For a moment, Miss didn't know what to say. Then she remembered, 'What was in the parcel, Verona?'

'This!' Verona produced a woollen scarf in the official Fair Isle pattern of the Clovenhoof Star Fleet.

'May I see it?' Miss asked. She turned it over in her hands and stared at it closely. She was looking for a label – but there wasn't one.

Instead, there was a little tag with strange markings on it. If you could read Sheepish, you would know it said: *Made on Clovenhoof. Do not tumble dry.*

Royston, the Runaway Railway Cat

What rhymes with cat? You've got it – fat. And not many cats were as fat as Royston, the railway cat.

Royston liked to hang around the station. Every morning, lots of people caught the 07:44 train to London. And every evening, they arrived back at the station again. They would feed Royston with bits of sandwich, cheese, pie – you name it! Some of them would even make him little snacks specially.

Royston was very good at getting in the way. He liked to stretch out on the ticket office counter so that he blocked the hole in the window where you handed over your money. But nobody really minded. Even Mrs Timms, who wasn't especially fond of cats, bought her tickets from the machine outside so she wouldn't disturb him.

By and large – very large – he was a happy cat. His life might have gone on like that forever, with everyone making a fuss of him. But Royston had a secret dream: he wanted to go to London. He would watch the passengers boarding the train and he would think, *How exciting! Imagine seeing Big Ben ... and Tower Bridge ... and Buckingham Palace!*

Very slowly (because 'quickly' wasn't really a Royston word) an idea began to grow between his rather tatty ears, behind his green eyes and inside his big jet-black head.

A cat's got to do, he said to himself, *what a cat's got to do*.

So one morning, at exactly 07:42, he jumped down from his usual spot on the counter, stretched his legs and yawned.

'Where are you off to, Royston?' said the inspector. But Royston just sauntered onto the platform, plonked himself down and started washing his face.

'The train now arriving at Platform One,' went the announcement, 'is the 07:44 for London.'

The passengers didn't notice Royston as he slipped between their legs and into the carriage. To his left was the standard class compartment. *Hmm, looks a bit cramped,* he thought. To his right was first class with its roomy seats and air conditioning. It was almost empty. *That's more like it!* thought Royston. He nipped inside and jumped onto a seat by the window. *No sweat!* he said to himself.

But an inspector was standing on the
platform and was amazed to see Royston's
chubby face peering out of the window.

'*Stop*!' he shouted to the station manager,
who was about to blow his whistle. 'Royston's
on the train!' And Royston was quickly
swept up from his comfortable seat and
dumped (rather rudely he thought) back
on the platform.

Any other cat might have given up at this point – but not Royston.

He noticed that most of the men on the train wore suits. Just outside the station were some recycling bins; one was for old clothes. That night, Royston jumped into the bin and rummaged around. He clambered out again, dragging an old suit behind him. *This'll do nicely!* he purred.

The next morning, nobody noticed when he slid under the ticket barrier – even though the arms and legs of the suit were far too long and dragged on the ground behind him.

A lady was waiting on the platform with her two white poodles. One of them spotted Royston and whimpered, 'What is *that*?'

'What?' growled the other one. Then he saw the huge suit creeping towards him. 'Oh, *dogness me*!' he yelped. 'It's a *ghost*!' And they shot off down the platform, dragging their owner behind them.

Royston
hopped onto
the train. He'd
only just sat down
when a lady jumped
up and screamed,
'Guard! There's a
horrid old tramp sitting
in first class! Get rid of him
immediately!' And ten seconds
later, Royston was got rid of.

This time, any other cat would definitely have given up. But Royston noticed that first class passengers all carried newspapers. So the next morning, he put on his suit and grabbed a newspaper from a rubbish bin.

When he sat down in the train, he opened the newspaper and held it in front of his face. Nobody noticed that he was just a fat black cat, and the train set off for London.

Result! purred Royston.

London wasn't just big – it was HUMUNGOUS! Royston had never seen so many people. He almost got trampled by the crowds. A pair of city mice pointed at him and laughed at his suit until they cried.

'Watch it!' he growled. 'Mouseburgers are very popular where I come from!'

He sneaked into the back of a London taxi. The taxi driver threw him out near Buckingham Palace. Royston suddenly remembered an old nursery rhyme:

Pussycat, pussycat, where have you been?
I've been up to London to visit the Queen.

That's an epic idea! he thought. And when the guards' backs were turned, he scampered through the gates and into the palace grounds.

A lady tourist from Norway tapped a policeman on the shoulder. 'Excuse me! A tiny, tiny gentleman in a big, big suit has just run into your Queen's house!'

'Thank you, madam,' he smiled. 'I will certainly bear that in mind.'

Royston wandered around until he found an open window. He leapt onto the window sill – then tripped over a trouser leg and landed in a heap on the floor.

He seemed to be in someone's bedroom – someone very rich. Instead of an ordinary light bulb, there was a huge crystal chandelier, and on the head of the bed was carved a golden crown.

The bed was big – but not quite king-sized.

London is very interesting, thought Royston as he jumped onto the bed, *but also very tiring*. He curled up on the soft velvet bedspread and fell asleep.

The next thing he heard was a lady's voice. 'Philip! Come and see! There's an extremely small person asleep on my bed!'

'Goodness gracious!' said a man's voice. 'How very peculiar!'

Royston looked up and yawned, half asleep.

'It's a *cat*!' exclaimed the lady and the man together.

Royston blinked at them. The lady was short and wore pink pyjamas and a golden crown, like the one on the bed-head. The man was tall and thin. Royston thought he'd seen them both before, but he couldn't think where.

'Have you come far?' enquired the man.

'He's a cat, Philip,' said the lady. 'I don't suppose he speaks English. Now, why don't you nip along to the kitchen, dear, and get him some milk?'

The man came back without any milk –
but with a whole bowl of fresh cream instead.
Right then and there, Royston decided that
he would stay in the palace and live with the
nice lady and the man.

And you never know, Royston thought, *one
day I might even meet the Queen*.

Baxter, the World Bear

Baxter was a polar bear. He lived at the North Pole. One day, he told the other bears, 'I'm heading south.'

'You don't want to do that,' warned one old bear. 'That's what your dad did, and he never came back.'

'Exactly,' said Baxter. 'And I'm going to find him.'

The old bear shook his head. 'They say the further south you go, the less cold it gets – until it's so uncold that the ground turns to water and the land turns green.'

'That's fine by me!' Baxter replied. 'I'm sick of white! The ice is white; the ground is white. Snow? White. Clouds? White. Baby seals? White. Seagulls? White. Even we're white! I don't care if the ground turns orange with purple spots!'

The old bear sighed and gave him a big red compass. 'Just follow the needle,' he said, 'and you're bound to go south.'

Baxter said goodbye, then trotted quickly away from the camp.

Soon he came to a signpost. It read:

South Africa: 11,000 miles

South Dakota: 4,000 miles

Southend: 3,000 miles

He pointed at the places in turn, chanting, 'Eeny, meeny, miny musk, catch a walrus by the tusk ... Southend it is, then – wherever that is!'

Baxter made up a song and he sang it loudly as he walked:

'They say that the sun always shines in the West
And a bear can go strolling in shorts and a vest,
And white is unknown in the colourful East
Where pink and blue snow isn't odd in the least,
But of all the directions a bear can explore
The South is the one I completely adore!'

As Baxter headed south, he noticed that the weather was definitely getting uncolder. Then, suddenly, he reached the end of the world. He peered over the edge of a cliff of ice into the deep blue sea.

'Bother!' he said. 'So the ground really does turn to water. I can't go back now – everyone will laugh at me.'

Then there was a loud crack! A huge chunk of ice had broken off from the land and was floating out to sea – and Baxter was sitting on it. Already the gap was too big for him to jump, and soon the land disappeared altogether.

The next day, it was even more uncold. Half of Baxter's iceberg had melted away. 'Double bother!' he said. 'If this goes on, I'll have to swim.'

In the middle of the night, he woke with a start. Bump! The iceberg had hit something hard.

It was Scotland.

He climbed ashore and walked straight into a big wooden sign. It read:

John O'Groats
Welcomes
Careful Bears

Land's End: 1,000 miles
Southend: 700 miles

Baxter peered at his compass and set off towards the South.

Soon, he heard a great roar behind him.
Something with two huge, burning eyes was
chasing him! He broke into a run but it was
no good – the roaring grew louder and soon
the eyes were right behind him.

Then a friendly voice said, 'Hop in, pal! I'll
give you a lift!'

Baxter had never seen a car before.

'Where are you heading?' the driver asked.

'Southend,' replied Baxter.

'How strange!' laughed the driver. 'So am I!' He added, 'We don't get many polar bears around here.'

'I'm not a polar bear,' Baxter explained. 'I'm a *world* bear.'

As they drove south, it became more and more uncold and the land turned more and more green. At first Baxter enjoyed the warm air, but then he began to feel too warm. 'It's, um, very ... uncold,' he told the driver.

'No problem,' he replied. 'I'll open the window.'

The next day, it was even more uncold.

'No problem,' said the driver. 'I'll put the roof down.'

When they reached Southend, Baxter felt as if he was going to boil. There were people everywhere. When they spotted Baxter, they all shouted and pointed. This cheered him up a bit and he waved back.

The driver dropped him off at the beach. He decided to take a walk on the pier where a cool sea breeze was blowing. There didn't seem to be quite so many people around now. Baxter wondered where they had all gone.

To tell the truth, he was a little disappointed. He'd come an awfully long way to see the South and although it was quite nice, it wasn't – you know – *that* nice ...

He went into the Tourist Information office. 'Excuse me,' he said. 'Is this the end of the South?'

'N-n-n-no,' said the lady behind the desk. 'There's lots more south, down ... ' – and she pointed into the distance – 'south.'

'So why's it called Southend then?' demanded Baxter.

The lady frowned. 'Good question.'

Baxter sighed. 'I suppose I'd better go even further south.'

Baxter got to France. It was even bigger than Southend. Baxter had hardly eaten anything since he left the Arctic, and he was getting very hungry indeed.

His mouth watered as he stared through the window of a busy restaurant. A waiter saw him and beckoned. '*Monsieur*! Please come in!'

Baxter sat down and looked at the menu. He ordered something called steak Béarnaise[1] because he thought it might be for bears. It wasn't. It was horrible. *It's no good*, he thought sadly. *I'll have to go even further south.*

---

[1] Steak Béarnaise is cooked steak with an eggy sauce. Baxter would have preferred steak tartare, which is much nicer for bears because it's raw.

In Africa, it was so uncold that all the water had turned to ground, and poor Baxter was terribly thirsty. 'This is unbearable!' he complained. 'I'll just have to go further south.'

Day after day, he followed the needle on his compass until he reached the sea. 'Phew!' he said, mopping his brow. 'About time, too!'

In the harbour was a boat; Baxter climbed aboard. The long walk had tired him out, and he soon fell asleep.

When he awoke, the boat was bobbing on the ocean and Africa was nowhere to be seen. But when he looked at his compass, he saw he was still heading south.

Every day, it grew less uncold until one day, a huge whale leapt out of the sea and soaked him with cold water. Big white seagulls circled overhead.

'This is more like it!' Baxter cried.

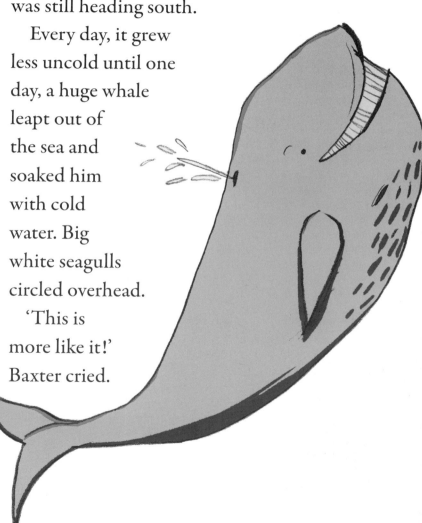

Then one morning, Baxter saw a thin white line in the distance. As he drew closer, he saw it was a shining cliff of ice. For the first time since he'd left the Arctic, he felt truly happy.

On the shore, a wooden sign read:

Antarctica,
home of the penguin
(NOT the polar bear)

Baxter realized how lonely he was. He hadn't spoken to another bear for a whole year.

'Hello!' he cried. 'Anybody home?'

Suddenly he heard a shout. 'Hello! Bear ahoy!' And out of a snow cave popped a big white, shaggy head.

'Dad!' cried Baxter. 'It's *me*!'

And they flung their arms around each other and danced for joy.

'Blimey, Son,' said Baxter's father. 'You took your time! I've been hanging around here for months!'

'How did you know I'd come?' asked Baxter, cuddling up to his dad.

'Oh,' his father replied, 'it's in our blood. We pretend we're world bears, but we have to travel to the other end of the world to find out that really, we're *very much* polar bears! Now you're here, we'll set off for home at once. Come on!'

'Oh, Daaaad!' moaned Baxter. 'I've only just got here! At least let me ... Oh, never mind!'

About the author

I've always loved writing. I've written true stories about running across the Sahara Desert and about diving with tiger sharks. So why did I write three stories about travelling animals? It's because they're also true – well, almost.

Royston the cat is really a ginger tom called Max who lives at my local railway station. Baxter is based on a polar bear I met once in a café in Oxford. He told me he'd lost his bearings. As for Verona's sheep, well, everyone knows that sheep are really aliens. Don't they?